# INTERIOR
# NIGHT

# INTERIOR NIGHT

John Stammers read philosophy at King's College London and is an Associate of King's College. His first collection, *Panoramic Lounge-bar*, was awarded the Forward Prize for Best First Collection 2001 and shortlisted for the Whitbread Poetry Award 2001. His second collection, *Stolen Love Behaviour*, was a Poetry Book Society Choice. He was Judith E. Wilson Fellow at the University of Cambridge. He is a creative writing tutor and freelance writer. He lives in Hampstead, London, with his wife and their two sons.

*Also by John Stammers*

Panoramic Lounge-bar
Buffalo Bills
Stolen Love Behaviour

John Stammers

# INTERIOR
# NIGHT

*Peter,*

*best wishes,*

*[signature]*

PICADOR

First published 2010 by Picador
an imprint of Pan Macmillan, a division of Macmillan Publishers Limited
Pan Macmillan, 20 New Wharf Road, London N1 9RR
Basingstoke and Oxford
Associated companies throughout the world
www.panmacmillan.com

ISBN 978-0-330-51338-8

1 3 5 7 9 8 6 4 2

A CIP catalogue record for this book is available
from the British Library.

Printed by CPI Mackays, Chatham ME5 8TD

Visit **www.picador.com** to read more about all our books
and to buy them. You will also find features, author interviews and
news of any author events, and you can sign up for e-newsletters
so that you're always first to hear about our new releases.

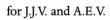

for J.J.V. and A.E.V.

# Acknowledgements

Acknowledgements are due to the editors of the following publications in which some of these poems first appeared: *Blinking Eye, London Review of Books, Poetry Daily, Poetry London, Poetry Review*. 'Funeral' was first published in *Identity Parade: New British and Irish Poets* (Bloodaxe, 2010) ed. Roddy Lumsden.

'A Pause on a Landing' was commissioned for an exhibition at Shandy Hall (Laurence Sterne Trust) alongside a tapestry of the same name by Patrick Caulfield. This was based on a passage from *Tristram Shandy* (Volume IV, Chapters 8–13) where Tristram's father Walter and his uncle Toby pause on a landing after Walter has been bemoaning the damage done to his son's nose during birth. 'Afternoon Tuesday' was commissioned for *19 Raptures*, a series of leaflets by various authors and artists produced for RAPt (The Rehabilitation of Addicted Prisoners Trust), www.rapt.org.uk, by Neal Brown. 'The Coolerator' is an extended extract from an article by Charles F. Eckhardt, used with permission.

Thanks are due to The Royal Literary Fund for its support during the writing of this book. Thanks are also due to Don Paterson for his criticism, advice and support and to Mark Waldron for his suggestions on the text.

# Contents

# INTERIOR
# NIGHT

# Funeral

I too know it, the charm of funerals in the rain,
the ferocity of a veil in daylight
or the studied black suits and millinery:
disremembered rituals of the tribe.

The portals of the mausoleum lean
as if having suffered break-ins
by morbid archangels;
its columns evince a certain verticality,
each finding itself unable to fall
into that abstraction
known as giving up the ghost.

Wreathes sadden in a damp mode.
I smoke an ugly brown cigarillo;
its liverous grey wisps swell the nose.
We shall float up, a grey twist of smoke.
Are you with me, yourselves, at the rendezvous?

# Ondine

Tonight I want to listen to the rowdiest music. Strike up
the timpani, O timpanist! The oboe and the flute
are an arranged marriage, but one that works.

                           I have fallen for the second cello
again. Can she see me listening to her bowing?

Who am I today, fashioned from my memories of happiness?
'Why?' is the oddest word. It brings into being the possibility of
a reason which there may not be. But why so?

                                I am fraught with answers.

I won't be that person they all make piteous remarks about
when he leaves the party – all those pose-junkies
laden with their own views of themselves.

                             Remember Lionel
who bought that minute gallery in somewhere?
And Doreen who can't hold down a man . . . ?

I am going to train to be a ballet dancer just for the noise
the feet make over the stage. But the set is chaos!
Stay away from colours, designer.

How extensive is an inkling? I believe I have one now
as the prima ballerina plots her way through the piece.

                             The curtain might part
and I would come dancing out.
Great acclaim in the reviews; great opprobrium in the
newspapers.

It might be possible for me to be fine
if I could live the way I hear the music when I'm not listening.

Once, when it didn't matter, I knew joy. It passed soon enough.

## Black Dog

From the inward night of the unconsciously tall arched doorway,
the shadows commence a faint unnerving undulation;
they wear an awful sheen, as if the shade has been interminably brushed
after being treated in some sciency new conditioner.
The aperture takes on shape: the hard sway of a long, high neck
and the absurd tiny slope of what, in another creature,
might have been its shoulders.
                            Black Dog,
some animal trader's corrupt attempt at a half-understood Swahili term,
his name is inked into him like a torturer's signature mark.
The single specimen they ever found, a male giraffe
black as the whitest sunlight, blacker
than the white crocuses in the ornamental flower-beds,
or the ultra-white of the open-eyed woman's white crêpe blouse.
It is merely a matter of waiting and everything happens:
the chimpanzees write Titus Andronicus on their toy typewriters;
the sea-lions bring down a gazelle;
the eels walk on two legs to the north gate and go home.
I feel a sensation of overwhelming disgust.
I make myself turn and leave the side of the enclosure.

# Afternoon Tuesday

It was complicated. We had brought the deal
over to Eddie's flat to bag it up into fives and tens.
But first we decided to try them. Not a thing.
Maybe they were chalk or a prescription remedy
for some not very serious condition. Bummer.
Better try some more. Some more, man. Nothing.
Few more. Get some drink. Put on the Underground. Louder!
Get some more drink. Ever thought about pottery, man?
Really interesting. Really. My friend Doug, he did pots,
not that small shit you do at school, big. Big . . .
No, man, vegetables. Think about it, they like just grow,
grow and you can't even stop them, they're like *alive* . . .
Ray's the first to hazard maybe they're working after all.
It's then that Eddie's Brenda shows up all pink
as if she's been banging the downstairs neighbour again.
Eddie glares like an attack dog in range of a miscreant.
Unsteady on her feet she sashays over to him,
cheeky and jollified, goes to sit on his lap –
'Hi hon', cat got your dick?' –
but misses slightly so she slides onto the floor
between him and the coffee table
wiping about a million tabs under the sofa.
'Jesus, Bren, watch that fat arse of yours!' says Ray.
'Don't take the Lord's name in vain *Raymondo*,
she says, 'specially not on the Sabbath.'
'It's Tuesday, you ridiculous lush,' he explains,
while I scramble under the sofa to get the pills.
And when I'm down there I pop another couple
or three which is what starts the row – a row that

strictly speaking, as it never ended, is still going on.
Somebody washed their hands of somebody else
a long time ago, and I for one can't remember who.

# The Encounter of M.

I see you are here once more, my sweet.
Do you never think of that afternoon
in the ornamental garden? The sun was low
and we cast long shadows over the plush white lawn;
the large topiary pyramids cast no shadows.
I called you my Louise. You wore
a little black dress. I was in dinner suit.
We had breakfast. We drank
lemonade with Benedictine and brandy
and ate quails' breasts on dry toast
with soft-boiled eggs. We were lovers.
You were the shade of my heart.
You said you would come with me, live with me.
I never saw you again until now, this afternoon
here in the ornamental flower garden.
I do not know you, sir, and would be grateful
if you would be so kind as to let me alone.
I find it tiresome practically to the point of death
to be approached by a stranger in dinner-dress.
It is, after all, the afternoon before breakfast.
And I could never take a lover. Leave me be
here in the long, black shade from the pyramids of topiary.
Permit me to introduce myself, I am M——.
And who are you, young lady, with your black bob
so Louise Brooks annealed in black and white?
I confess to you that I find your black dress
and white silk scarf with its black polka-dots entrancing.
It is rather late in the afternoon.
This is my first time here. How charming
the ornamental flower garden is

with these geometric topiaries
that seem to throw no shadow. I see that you and I
cast long, dark shadows. It is early in the day.
M., do you not know me? You called me
Louise B. You loved my blunt bob and bangs
and the defiant chic of my little black dress.
You said I was your heart's shadow.
You offered me a way out. A way out, you said.
We walked in this ornamental garden
and stood on the lush, green lawn
beside the huge topiary pyramids. They cast
long, opaque shadows. We had no shadows.
We drank brandy and Benedictine
and fresh lemon pressé. We suppered
on quails' eggs and herring roes.
So you have returned, my dear M.
Do you recall that afternoon here
in the ornamental garden? The sun was high
and we cast no shadow across the green lawns;
the pyramids of hedgework cast elongated shadows
like beaks of vast black birds across our path.
You used to call me L.B. I wore a white silk dress
a little too modish, I thought, for daywear. You
were dressed in morning suit and white tie.
We took a little breakfast. We drank
mint tea with lime and Champagne
then ordered poached turbot with samphire
and hard-boiled eggs. We were lovers.
You said you would take me, be with me.
I never saw you again until now, this afternoon
in the ornamental flower garden.
My dear lady, may I beg your pardon.

I am afraid you have the advantage of me.
I am delighted, however, to be misidentified
by so beautiful a young woman.
You look so . . . so Louise Brooks
stood out against the black and white shadow.
I see we cast no shadow here
by the deep black shade of the topiary pyramids.
Shall we take afternoon tea?
I have ordered lemon tea and soft-boiled eggs
and cucumber florets with triangles of toast for us.
I love you. Take me. I love you. Come with me.
You are the shadow of my heart! Yes. Yes!
We will drink Champagne and Beaumes de Venise and dine
on ortolan and Black Sea caviar and golden samphire.
My dearest, I see you are here once more.
Do you ever think back to that afternoon
in the ornamental flower garden?
The sun was low and we cast no shadows
across the plush white lawn.

# A Pause on a Landing

*(the birth of Tristram Shandy)*

Small item, Trismegistus thou never wert!
Arrived twixt the observance and the breech,
your new-minted proboscis is magenta and corrupt.
You will be said to have a *nose*.
O rude appropriation
from the eternal birthing bed of nought
to this passing birthday of sunlight and gloom!
It is well said that the sins of the forefathers
are visited on the faces of the sons.
Vociferous little Shandyling, be not anxious.
It is but a pause on a landing,
a momentary inhalation
replete with nosegay and reek,
then the long bed once more.

# Interior Night

Stunned by an iron-black fatigue, I am a man driven mad mental
by a woman I'll never meet. I stagger stock-still
beneath the poster for Supernature by Goldfrapp.
Across the tubelines is her semi-nude music advert.
Someone's daughter shed her clothes for that ad –
or never put them on – in the name of art:
the art of getting really famous so that strange men
slake their concupiscence on you on tube platforms.
I adore her high cork-heeled shoes.

The unshaven, Caledonian guitarist
sings the Dancer at the Gate of Death,
or something which sounds oddly like that,
fierce and obscurely irreconcilable
with any imaginable dance-manoeuvres.
He hammers the strings like a slaughtering drum,
repetitious and bleakly sardonic,
to the commuter girls' heel-strike
like so many chisels on high-end, black marble.

This is a day for jumping. This is not a day
for jumping under; it is a day for jumping into
the moment that is gone before landed in,
into that arriving thwack which will rush me off
to the end of the line and all points connecting.
The rails boom to the oncoming train, plosive along the line
to fuck-knows-anywhere-actually, further even.
Travelling back and forth is its own form of stasis.
*'On attend le Metro,'*

a Frenchwoman outlines to her little girl.
The resonance pounds in the gaps between noise
as the sound survives the death of the song
and the fluorescents judder with delayed silences.
Consider the interiority of a coal-grey rat,
purposeful knowing no purpose,
that scurries between the tracks of disused lines.
Invisible rain crashes from the inner sky.
It always comes down to this:
I am at the gate along a black tunnel.
My personality lacks all cohesion. I am in fragments.

Thank heavens for you at least, Alison Goldfrapp
and your half-naked advert, your unconscionably elongated legs,
the bare back of your bent wrist held fastidiously
in place of your breast in a faux-breast, more breast than breast
as these devices tend to be. Alison,
I could wait at the end of line for you,
for the exact pair of doors to slide fully across, to open
so that I might enter manfully and with a true conviction.

The twin black holes of the tunnel-ends
suck the platform out like a flat, deflatable universe
in the same way that the whole lunatic edifice
will itself be sucked back to nought, the abiding nought.
All things die, and when you die you're dead. End of.

# Once

*i.m. M.D.*

I have never seen you stand more gracefully
than at the corner of the new century
when we were expecting portents and encountered
merely the slow, somnolent march of young men,
the hell-bent kind, as they moved across
into full disillusionment with no more than a wince.

Your strained countenance announced for us all
the right attitude to strike: that of the wounded
in a land of thorough well-being. You were like Christ
on one of his last visits home, before he departed
for his Father's house somewhere over the clouds,
which might be Nebraska or the Sea of Japan
or any one of those alternative heavens
we have come to adore from the travel posters.

I, for one, never doubted you. You madman.
Never once thought you were anything other
than what you allowed your devotees to claim you to be.
I have known genius and I have known lunacy
and this was a kind of genius for lunacy.
When you fell, you made sure it was a long, long way.

# Film in a Time of Rages

Nowhere is so sad as a cinema full of light.
He watches the houselights go up on rows of seats
with no one in them. The velour of them.
The cute numbers on their tiny plaques.
In a fall of anthem and the hushed, respectful egress
of an audience, the picture house
has slowly come to a halt. He pauses to take in
the mysterious face of his wristwatch
as it smears the time away in large sweeps.

Pathé News is all the rage in an era
with more than enough rage for it to be the all of.
He has sat through the shambles of Northern Europe,
the newsreel of carnage and ordnance
presented as information on something else.
How is he to respond to fresh news of death?
Compassion enough was early in his life
but the arc of his empathy had nose-dived
through the course of events.
For a moment the world across the Channel
floats for him as if on a child's inflatable globe,
the countries demarcated by pale colours
and the outlines of national jurisdictions.
What was a child's death in A, a political fact
or a sociological fact or a fact constructed?

At such moments he is thrown back
onto astrophysics or ancient Greek thinkers
who wore their considerable barrels lightly.
In the long run our noisy tenancy

will lapse. In the very long run our world
would. In the very, very . . . he stops himself
thinking about it in terms of runs,
whatever they might be. He feels oddly light-headed
with the notion of a complete void
in place of all this stuff, as if he and everyone else
were already consumed and this
was a kind of after-echo or ghost image
as when a powerful light source goes out.
These are the days when radar is all the rage,
when a downed, spectral aircraft will live on
as a green smudge on a vectored screen,
the way that same smudge will live on
in the mind of the screen's operative
who in turn, and so forth. It was doubtless
a question of runs, he thought.

This was during the V-1s, as they called it.
Three doors away down his street
kingdom came in the form of a rocket
that blew several neighbours to it.
He saw the same thing portrayed
in a feature film. It didn't look as grotesque
as he reckoned it must have been.
Their remains were never excavated,
he assumed because there were none.
People made do with a ceremony
which he had come to see would outlast –
because not material and so timeless –
any vestige or substantial residue.
Did the people know this? Should he tell them?

He felt it was really up to the government.
He stepped from the picture house
into the cinematic glare of full daylight,
the rage of a siren and a buzzing
he suddenly prayed not to hear the end of.

# Existential

When we designed the world we found it necessary
to leave room for the absences.
You will notice there is a good deal more emptiness
than objects. This ensures that when an item
passes out of existence it may be accommodated.
It would be more correct to say that the world is composed
both of the things that are and the things that are not.
The same holds true for people. When a person passes
they become a void precisely equivalent to themselves.
In a regrettable misapprehension, there are those who believe
they can in some way perceive the lost ones.
They give names to such things: ghosts, spirits, visitations.
I assure you they cannot; they that are gone
are gone for good and all, and are manifestly absent
in every way. So much will surely now be obvious:
otherwise they would be unable to occupy
that particular non-existence corresponding to the former them.
Since the beginning these spaces have continued
to grow in number with no sign of abatement.
It is our conclusion, therefore, that in the end
the whole of existence will be a single miraculous absence.

# O

I hear no songbird's breath, see no scent of lily flowers.
From two brass pipelets and one plastic bong
shift blue-grey coils of smoke. In an upstairs spare room
are faces congealed into faintly visible questions
or epiphanies stillborn at the point of emergence.
This bedsit miasma is merely the latest form
to materialize from your opium trial. Before this,
you have crumbled the opulent, black truffle
to boil above the candle's slight flame,
half-baked lab work to extract a tacky, mauve liquor.
The mosquito stab of the hypodermic has pumped
the little thrill of injection down your plump vein.
You wish an arm of glass to see the relief slide in.
Breathe. Breathe and feel it like an orgasm held perpetually
at the instant of climax. Give it to me. Please.

But when the goods might be, the fleet, pseudo-adrenal
charge of blood chemistry excited to unnatural heat,
there is no more than a kind of blunt vacancy.
I feel nothing; they feel nothing; we feel nothing.
We conjugate a blank consensus: this stuff doesn't work.
We mumble soft complaints on the futility
of doing this so-called drug with its sorry rigmarole:
we are children of the amphetamine generation!
Nothing is happening, nothing: no rush, no burn,
no ecstasy of transport; why are we still
in this room after how many hours has it been after?

Decades later it finally hits, as the recollections surface
and re-swell like tissue-paper flowers in a water glass:
that's the whole beautiful reason of it. Peace for the wicked.
Now the sweet O never bubbles to a purple gunge on the spoon.
These days you live with neither rush nor tranquillity,
just obscure head pain and proprietary codeine.

## Nightsweats in the Afternoon

I had lain beneath the thin gauze of the afternoon,
stare-eyed through the siesta hours
when the sky beats out a red glow like hot coals
and my insides fever with a need.
I get up thirsting from these non-sleeps,
wrestle up out of my bed
the way a forest moth squeezes itself
wriggling, eyeballs-out, from its cocoon.
Whoever invented the mosquito net
had a finely-tuned appreciation of boundaries.

Times like these I seek out the kitchen,
its long, wide screens slid fully back,
oblongs of wet tropical air into the room.
The light from the ice-box fans out like a cone
and me outlined in its exact beam.
I am so awake at these moments,
without a hint of sleep or indistinctness
as if energised with light and the cold air
flowing out and over me.
It might be heaven
or the fabrication of a diseased mind.

Happy-hour for the miserable.
The ceiling fan slaps the saturated air;
the rattan window-screens tick,
their fibres constrict like field-hospital sutures.
Behind me, the bar's screen door snaps closed
like a fly trap onto an incautious wasp.
A young woman at the far end of the room grinds her ass

backwards into her gentleman-friend's groin
to the sound of a tinny Latino radio station,
runs a hand through her long greasy hair.
He slides his grimy outstretched fingers
all up and down her bare arms.
The defunct volcano rises above the succulent rainforest;
the locals call it the Old Man.

On the clouded, flaking bar mirror
a line of tepid water inches down.
I look past the bar steward's shoulder.
Between the mirror's green, appliquéd palm fronds
I see an older version of myself
in soiled cheesecloth shirt and cracked linen jacket.
When would I grow that beard?
The hired help take flat-eyed looks at me from time to time,
mutter to one another in their own language.

Jameson's with a dilemma of ice –
a single cube scrapes in the bowl of my glass.
I take a hard pull; my back straightens;
I begin to believe in my own genius once again.

## In a Time of Great Moment

the minutes have quite a job to do. I lay back and assess
the glowing red numerals on the radio alarm clock as they pause
between instants.

I have expected a lethal occurrence since early adulthood
                                    and have felt greatly let down
by my good fortune.
                                    The least piece of danger
has scoffed in my face – ain't he the lucky one, it would muse.

                                    When I think of Howard Hughes
I cannot escape the conclusion that he tried to vitiate his
failure with a show of aplomb. Then the opposite.
                                    Those entrepreneurs!

# The Woman

As if she has been called away from a superb party,
a woman sits in a shaded corner;
the brim of her wide hat cuts a twice-dark shadow
across her face like a thick, purple brushstroke.
I am in a vacant house like that of an enormous family
who once occupied a hundred rooms.
I feel a touch on my arm. I look about the room.
There is no one else. The touch remains.

Faded, covered armchairs hold the impression of a weight
like a lost comfort; the bed is layered by the past.
The chair she sits upon is of woven silk
and a deep, polished hardwood.
I reach up for a curtain and pull it to me
as if there might be written on it instructions
as to how to implicate one another
in a conspiracy of the huge unnatural house.

I am in a guest-room I have lost the memory
of why I am occupying. A wedding? A christening?
There is a sumptuous shifting noise;
her thighs kiss like delicate lesbians.
Is this deviance? Any experience is infected
with the germ of its own desire. I mean demise.
I feel a further touch on my arm, twice
like the soft, double contact of a gloved hand.

She wears her astonishing body like a living map
of the erogenous. I look up to the bright ceiling

of a curved alcove I know to be square.
My head draws back. The curve is the upper edge
of a white lampshade in the foreground.
Still the sense of touch. Things order themselves
according to an unstated emotional principle.
She motions touch me, don't touch me.

# Like a Heatwave Burning

It was the hottest summer on record;
we flew into rages at the drop of a pin.
The heat made cacti of us all.

I woke up hot crazy at one in the morning.
The day's sun had heated up the sky so heavy
it felt like being ironed.

We sat on the curbside like hot bananas
and Jane read me the Miranda
of our future lives together:

there would be no future lives together.
I'd never heard the nightjay squawk
so damnably shrilly in the still, still stilly.

My eyeballs made sinuous rills.
I sloughed on my sandals and loped
onto a streetcar named expire.

Tyres welded cars to the road.
I got out my character
and began the tasks of a lifetime.

Pine trees collapsed in a dead swoon
all over the place. Believe you me,
honeydew features, it was hot.

# The University

A brown paper carrier-bag stands
upright and open in the hallway
like a manhole. He places objects
for later into the bag. The brown
street door leads off a long front passage
with brown paintwork.
A small brown spider walks across the wall.
He goes out to acquire another object.
The street goes downhill in both directions.
In the terraced street are smoke-blackened houses;
not a motor car or bicycle goes by.
One motor car is parked at the far end
almost at the limit of vision.
A brown sun is a flat light.
He walks up to the corner shop.
The corner juts at an unnatural angle.
He is going to go to the university
in a different street to start
and find out what happens.
He walks past the grey post box
with its rectangular mouth.
He picks up a can of baked beans
from the corner shop. No one is in
the corner shop. Nothing is on the shelves.
In the hallway he places the tin of beans
in the brown paper carrier-bag.
The terraced houses are thick with smoke;
they have a grey-brown tinge. The walls are damp.
He puts another object into the carrier-bag.
He takes something out of the carrier-bag.

He will take the brown paper carrier-bag
to the university which is in the other street.
The sun throws a vague daylight,
the shadows of the lampposts are bent over double:
they are now upside-down coat hooks.
He opens the front door from the unlit hallway.
A clear light-bulb hangs in the front passage.
The stiff brown paper carrier-bag is open.
There is nothing in the brown paper carrier-bag.
He goes out the front door
into the smoke-black terrace.
At the university he will study.
The street goes uphill in both directions.
He walks downhill to the corner shop.
There is no corner shop.
He returns to the house with a tin of soup.
The hallway recedes in extreme perspective.
A large brown spider walks down
the kitchen wall and onto the worktop.
There is no motor car in the street.
The bicycle is chained to the front railings.
He opens a pint of milk in the back kitchen.
The milk is sour. He goes to the corner shop
and brings back a half pint bottle of beer.
He places a pint of milk in the carrier-bag.
The university is in another street.
From the long, black hallway
he opens the black front door.
The brown paper carrier-bag is empty.
He picks it up and places it back where it is.

## The Débâcle

The lounge room was cleared well in advance.
Our Filipina maid, whom we call Desultora
when she isn't listening – which seems to be all the time –
was dressed up prettily all in black.
I had got home three hours early to assist with "putting out".
A whole salmon was spread over a whole salver
supplied with it by our fish merchant,
it being so long. Nibbles in bowls on every surface.
Veronica made precise little hippopotamuses out of green olives.
My best Hermitage had been set to breathe, the Chablis chilled.
All forty-three guests arrived exactly on time.

# By a Shining Light

I thought I saw my mother garlanded.
In a yellow pinny and cream twin-set,
her pearls were the sound of cymbals and bells.
She stood in a powerful, colourless light.
All around her the light shone.
I looked up, there was no below me,
and I reached up my arms to her and she was above me.
Speaking, she spoke words that were sounds
I could not understand, but were filled
with a great significance.
At once I was reassured
and an immense happiness flowed over me
like a baptism in the river Jordan.
And I went to speak to her, to say . . .
I do not know what it was I would have said,
but the words came out as odd cries.
Then nothing and my room was dull
and I was a grown man and forgotten.

# Out of My Depth

I know this is lunacy. I came across, in the gutter,
a wet ball of paper. I picked and picked at it
until writing in bled, watery biro unwrapped.
The text pulled with such an odd nausea,
it seemed to be for my own attention.
And although it was the script that wavered,
it was me that sank. I sank

and it was as if, in some decrepit hospital bed
during the months of delusion and vomitus,
I'd be up there between the uncertain sway of two skyscrapers
on a high-wire, bang rigid, gripped
onto the short wavelength of a long pole,
or way, way out in a mid-ocean swell
barely treading water, below me the unfathomable abyss.

'Is he conscious?' they might be saying.
Yes, yes! I'm somewhere out here in the edgeless sea,
or I'm close to choking, sucked,
like the final minute in an hourglass,
into the dry quicksand of a dune marked:
DANGER DO NOT PLAY HERE!
One way or another, I'm going down.

The trees in my street gather in the wind,
and I could love them for their down-to-earthness;
there are neighbours behind those doors!
I look down into my own dear hands;
the words come open, simple, as the paper flattens.
These messages appear more frequently of late.

# Mr Punch in Soho

You would recognise that hook nose anywhere,
his hump and paunch, the shiny pink erection of his chin.
Withered, crossed legs on the barstool
dangle like transplants from a much smaller body.
He could have found his ideal slot in the Gestapo,
been a dab hand with a blinding iron.
And the scold's bridle would have been right up his Strasse.
He has, they say, killed seven police:
old-time rozzers on the beat
more deserving of a saucy come-on from the street girls
than the last rites down a back alley.
And two wives. Poor old Mrs Punch finally copped it
one night after he'd done a few dozen barley wines
and as many double gins. She fought fiercely
against an *assailant or assailants unknown*
the Pall Mall Gazette reported. Never caught.
Never charged. And pretty little Mrs Punch
number two won't be taking a bath
in those bubbles again. That's the way to do it!
Just picture him afterwards, cock in hand
like an old chimp with a hard, green-tipped banana.
And the baby, where's the baby?
It's something to make the Devil into the good guy:
how children cry out for him
to drag Punch down to hell for eternal punishment.
But he'd throttle Lucifer when his back was turned
and be back on that stool for closing time.
Or maybe that's where he's been all these years
of grown-up sleep, peaceful and free of nightmare.
It's what you can't see in the stare of his wooden yellow eye.
Don't look, there's his stick, the awful stick!

# The Theory of Flight

I became convinced of it only later.
I salvaged nylon sheeting from the burnt-out factory
at the end of the alley at the end of the next street.
Beneath an unwieldy canopy of rain and stormcloud,
I stretched it across the courtyard with large clamps
left over from my earlier experiments with retention.

The superstructure I wrangled from scaffolding poles
lifted in the small hours. These I bound
with disused electricity cables and a web of bungees,
frayed rope and torn bandage strips. I loved to hear the skin
stretch and screech in a painful flexion
as I larded it tight with layer upon layer of duct tape.

I became obsessed it would never be perfect,
like the contraptions of bolts, wires and glued-on remnants
of my other long-term engineering plans.
I would lie awake throughout the night in a cold fret
about the next stage of my latest enterprise.
On the radio discussion hour a lecturer described

how the theory of all theories dictates a paradox:
nothing can be all things without contradiction.
I reckoned this to mean that certain events
can be brought about by the force of pure logic alone
the way giant birds on clifftops command the wind.
If only I could imbue it with enough of the needful.

Throughout the breathless weeks of passion
I would stand at the back window –
the dull crack of thunder, the wet thud of lightning –

and behold its gigantic frame like an airborne whale-creature
that had crash-landed behind my building
out of some alternative system of evolution.

In a ritual benison, I tattooed a punk logo beneath the wings
to testify to an exotic philosophy of licence.
I woke up the next morning and it was gone.

# Rimbaud

(i) *His Stolen Heart*

He personifies his heart, already a metaphor,
says that he, his heart, is depressed
(defined as the prolonged absence of joy)
and that he mopes on the rails of a ship's poop deck.
Poop deck? That silly name for that sad look out:
*bonjour Trieste?*
The rude quodlibets of the rough crewmembers
sadden his heart further; he is covered in tobacco.
Covered in tobacco? Given up to tobacco as a symbol!

Those satyrophallic Jolly Jack Tars
with their figurative hard-ons and crude quodlibets
have seduced his heart with their obscene imaginings:
they have carved pornographic vignettes onto the ship's rudder
of all places! O ocean waves,
you abracadabra similes
like a child's innocent magic-word,
wash away their sex-filth, their anatomical profanities,
their naughty pictures from his personified mind!

So, when they've chewed their tobacco plugs –
the belches of Bacchus, god of the debauched,
erupt out of them like mini Etnas! – whither
stolen heart so duped by all that lewd stuff?
His stomach will have metaphorical somersaults
if he comes back besmirched (with tobacco, possibly).
So it's up to you, he says, to his personified heart,
when all this sex and tobacco silliness loses its allure.
So how about it, then, will you give it one more go?

## (ii) *Rimbaud's Rooks*

He is them as they beat down out of great skies;
they are him, his darling rooks, rooks his delight.
He dances them over the rock-hard winter farmlands
and the depressed hamlets
where matins bells no longer ring in the meadows
and to be or not to be is not the question.

He is a rook guerrilla general as he commands
the rook army of the severe cry
down the frozen, bilious backwaters
and the byways with their ancient stone crosses
like so many wayside Calvaries,
to mobilize, regroup, rally!

All above the fields of France,
seeded with the dead of other seasons,
he is convulsed to a furious thousand rooks,
harbinger birds in their death-black uniforms
who call the passing winter throng
to their duty as duty is their call.

But watchful, finally, he settles with them,
his soldiers of heaven among the oak tops,
understands to let be the dunnocks of May
in the hedgerows, to leave them for the weak ones
captive in the backwoods and the long grasses,
those forced to endure and no prospect of victory.

(iii) *Sa Bohème*

Beneath his personal mythy sky, in a fantasy
is our hero, his hands iced into his pockets,
the muse his one companion and confidante.

By day he saunters, his head a-brew with concoctions of poetry.
His sleep is full with love and amorousness, Oo là là!,
his very overcoat a mysterious magic garment.

A single pair of arse-out trousers has he,
the pauper prince, the revenant,
as from him tumble preposterous, unearthly lyrics.

The Zodiac is his gazebo whereunder pass nights of poesy;
there, possessed by every bohemian threnody,
the constellations dance rites and revels corybantic.

And on a September eve, the gossamer a-twinkle,
squatted by the roadside beneath the old lime trees
he listens with a cocked, purposeful ear,

his lovely forehead with a thin dew a-sparkle
like droplets of full, white Burgundy wine,
there he listens, yes, for the muse's gypsy-girl whisper.

It is then these lanes seem to him to thrum
with poems brought to him in a lunatic dance
by his supernatural counterpart,

as, with a hundred soft plucks and a tuneless hum,
he plays the bootlace of his burst *sabot* like a lyre,
his foot held close to his literal heart!

# Soft Cunt

You just got to do it, is all. It's one of those things.
It was really bitter that evening. It was November.
Raining like it always seemed to be at night
round our way at that time of year. And bitter.
Jimmy Collins was my best mate
but he always called me a soft cunt
right from when we was little. And then all the others
used to call me it as well. I fucking hated it.
I wanted to be hard. The best thing in the world
you could be was hard. Jimmy was hard.
It only happened because Jimmy's cousin
was at the same school as one of their lot.
And this other kid who was one of them
had said his brother'd seen me looking at him
and it was only because I was always with Jimmy.
But he'd fucking do me next time he saw me on my own.
So Jimmy says, 'Get in first. You gotta get in first.'
And if I did, I knew no one'd call me
a soft cunt again or look at me or nothing.
That night we all pile in the old Alma pub
at the end of the market which was still there then.
We had money from bits of burglary and thievery and that
and they knew us in there so we could always get served.
In the corner of the public bar was that old grandad
the one with the limp and old war medals
who was always in there with his half of Guinness
he'd ponced off one of the stallholders.
Stupid old fucker always going on about how
we never knew nothing and the war
and Chas, who was the comedian, says to him

'What fucking war was that, the Boer War?'
The Boer War! What a laugh! And old grandad
just says you had to be hard in the trenches, boy.
'That's enough of that, Corporal Jones,' Chas shouts at him,
and we all piss ourselves. Corporal Jones!
So we have a few and get a bit lagered-up anyway.
I had the flick-knife I'd got on our school trip to Jersey.
You could buy them there then. I never brought it out before.
Anyway, then we all bowl down to their flats
all shouting and all singing down the street
*Where are ya? Where are ya?*
like at the football with me and Jimmy out in front.
The way the blade went in him so easy
like he weren't there, like he'd already gone.
And he looks at me
like he's about to smile and I was his mate
or something and he's just seen me in the street.
Me, his mate! Silly fucker. What you smiling for?
But he never smiled, he made this sort of noise
and slumped down on his knees holding his chest.
Then I shouted at him
'Who you gonna *do* now? Who you gonna *do* now?'
Then one of the others shouts *Split!* and we legs it.
We got back to the bottom of C Staircase in our flats
where we always met up and that.
I was really fucking out of breath with running then I says,
'Did you see him! Did you see him!'
And as I say it I start giggling and can't stop.
And every time I go to say something
I just start giggling again and say 'Did you see him!'
and start giggling again, giggling. Then Jimmy says,
'For fuck sake stop giggling you soft cunt.'

# Vegas

The whole world fell in two and the night flipped open.
I pulled you from the wreckage of the day and into the casino.

We threw seven all night and laughed ourselves to sleep.

# The Coolerator

*West Texas*

The coolerator was a cabinet that looked a lot like an old-fashioned pie safe, but instead of having a wooden back and punched-tin sides and doors, the coolerator's back, sides, and doors were covered in fine-mesh screen wire. The top and bottom were solid, and the cabinet stood about a foot off the floor on spindly wooden legs. Each leg was immersed in a 1lb coffee can half full of kerosene. This kept crawling or climbing insects out of the coolerator. The screenwire sides and doors kept out the fliers. Inside there were three or four shelves for perishable foods.

The important part of the coolerator was not the cabinet, but that which kept it cool. A large pan, usually sheet metal, was placed atop the coolerator and filled about half way with water. A woollen blanket was draped over the pan, to hang all the way to the bottom of the coolerator cabinet on all sides. Often this was two or three threadbare woollen blankets sewn together, which would be used on beds in the winter. Atop the blanket, to sink it into the water, there was a brick or large rock.

The woollen blanket wicked the water down on all sides of the coolerator, and the ever-present Texas wind, blowing through the blanket, cooled the food inside through evaporation. With the coolerator set on a shaded but mostly-open porch, milk, butter, eggs, and other perishables stayed remarkably cool during the hot spring, summer, or fall of the year. With the coming of REA and electricity to rural Texas, coolerators and their kin vanished, to be replaced by electric refrigeration. They were not greatly missed.

# Bolton Southbound Platform

I was all washed up when I espied the Sir John Barbirolli
on a long run from John O'Groats
to God knows, infinity more than likely.
The hippie student girl
wore slinky hooped tights of black and pink,
a long smear of blue down the side of her hair
and a cute little pleated skirt.
She stood reading
*The Unbearable Lightness of Being*
and sported silver earphones. She was grooving on
some rock-chick Rock music, I presume.
O Mister Kundera, what will she do
when it takes her to the bridge?

For myself, I'd been rooted to this platform since circa 1972.
I was reeling in hopes and expectations
for the sexual revolution to fast sex
that never arrives. And lo!
I perceived that aforesaid bullet like a steely dan
thumping on down the trickerty-track, thumping,
and at that precise moment I finally knew
my true vocation:
I would give my life over
to the making of pornographic films
featuring college girls.

# The House Sale

Take your filthy cash and your Algerian finance;
leave my house alone, leave it, I'll let it to myself,
safe forever, secluded here in its serial pasts.
Buy it you bastard, buy it, but don't begin to try to possess it;
do not dare develop it, damn you, or a liking for it.
Give me what I want and I will wish you dead for doing so.
It is mine, I live here, die.

# The Shrine of Proteus

From an old fishermen's hut, unused and half derelict,
on our small, dry beach down past the marshes,
I took to myself a fancy to fashion a ruined temple.
On its inner walls I painted, in putrid greens and ghastly purples,
oversized images of barbarous sea gods that had never existed,
their deep-browed heads fringed with seaweeds and wrack,
lobe-heavy ears, vast, oceanic eyes and wide-toothed, open mouths.
Called into being too late for their own metaphysical significance,
in their secular false acropolis of parodical being
they nonetheless applied to their domain that imperious regard
which brooks no lack of devotional observance.
And so, at its centre, I placed an old concrete block
scratched over with red crayon as a sort of cod sacrificial altar.
It was all meant simply as a possible light diversion
for the boys and me during the big summer holidays.

For a week of hard flat sun which flayed the hours of long light,
in our make-believe shrine we played out unique ceremonies
of what we contrived to imagine as ancient Hellenic forms of worship.
Around the altarpiece we placed found items from the shore
and discarded or lost objects drained of their original affect
by casual disposal or the caustic action of the seawaters:
whin-feathered dune flowers, hardy but etiolated by the undercut
of salt breeze and the bitter, constant scratch of blown sand grains;
and two branches that the profound twist and torque of wave motion
had improbably transformed into twin horses of the deep.
I enjoyed particularly a blue, soft-toy man with a red topknot,
the kind in whose presence an infant will fall into sleep,
self-calmed, as it were, by its projected transitional warmth.

To him we assigned a special position beneath the painted idols:
a proxy man to be a continual supplicant in our absence.

We would, the three of us, pace endless circles around the centre stone
and sing ancient Greek phrases concocted from the Vocabulary of the
    boys' school primer:
*Bring us words thou gods of the ocean! Tell us truths of the deep!*
The boys would chant with that intense, unreasoning concentration
of a child, all hopeful that a sea oracle would respond with some sign:
a scrawled message writ in the sand by the tide, for instance,
or an eerie symbolic rearrangement of our simpleminded offerings.

Then one afternoon, quite unremarkable and fair as we thought,
we went down to our sacrificial hut and there in the corner, sat on the
floor, lent in a heap against the far wall, was an old, tattered man,
his lank grey hair and beard fallen like a silver waterflow over his
    shoulders and chest.
He wore about him this aged, shoddy, naval duffle-coat
secured around his broad waist with a line of twisted rope.
Beneath, he had on a thick Aran jumper, bitten with holes and rents,
and on his feet a pair of battered sandals tied on with odd bits of string.
His face peered out, a great polished segment of tree-trunk flotsam,
his vinous eyes, dark and acute with the gleam of two carnelians
and his mouth outlined by a pair of lips cracked with salt-white skin.

'Thank you, sirs,' he said, 'for the small consideration of this shelter.
I am wet with the sea. I am water soaked. I have salt in my veins.
I find myself for once, as you might say, captive, tethered to dry land.'
Being given to kind acts, as is my way, and the boys so obviously wrapt
to have this odd visitor in our fanciful play shed,
I agreed the old man should stay there a day or two to recover himself
to whatever level of vigour was habitual to him so he might move on,

the one absolute condition being that he confine himself to the
    rough shelter.
Those next days, the boys brought him sandwiches, half-bottles of ale
and leftovers from supper and pieces of cake, uncharacteristically
    forgone.

That last afternoon I remember we had gone to see our stranger.
He seemed well altered and had changed his garb, cut his beard
and on his head he wore a sailor's cap produced from somewhere.
Sensing their last chance perhaps, the boys set about to bind him
in the unyielding, iron chainwork of their childish enthusiasm
and compelling themselves, almost against their own reason,
for the very sake of the possibility of amazement, demanded
the old man – even as we had the graven deities around the walls –
impart to them some secret or spectacular wisdom of the sea.
And, as if fixed into a sudden trance, he responded thus:

'They have boiled the ocean, my boys, have poisoned the wide seas.
They have murdered the whale for glues and the octopi for sushi food;
they have rotted the deep sea-beds and defecated down the sea's throat.
I have seen the continental ice floes calving off the Antarctical shelf,
the infected heat of steam that rises unbid off the Malay straits,
and the huge sun fish horizontal at the surface for the want
of oxygenical water round an hundred Polynesian archipelagos.
But the great sea will boil 'em all, my boys, boil 'em,
as the acid rain eats the land, and man will fall upon man
and the one ocean will take its final reclamation.'

That night the weather at last shelved in with black stormclouds;
the coast trees pulled at their own branches as if in some awful distress;
the cast and glare of lightning grazed the horizon with sickly
    grey bruises.

All at once there was unleashed a tempest of such curious ferocity
it was barely precedented, even in our volatile Channel waters.
The boys were wretched with concern for the old loony down at
    the beach.
But there was nothing to be done. I assured them our antique shed
was solid built and had stood for years through multiple downpour,
    gale and hurricane,
not to say the Luftwaffe's aerial bombardment of the adjacent docks.

That next morning we flew as if wing-footed down to our hut.
Nothing remained of our sea chapel or the strange man,
only the roil of the tide all about us as it dismantles granite to sand
and, on our altar, the saturated corpse of the blue child's man-doll.
The boys were convinced beyond any logic that I could summon
that the raggedy sailor was some kind of sea-god of antic myth.
I was compelled to punish them that night for going too far
in their silliness. And I would have beaten the old sea dog
who had set their minds into such a ferment, had I been able.
There are boundaries I will not have violated.

# Paris Anywhere

He was muttering lines of symbolist poetry as he sat on the end of the iron bed; the Eiffel Tower creaked marginally on its grand pivot, an inaudible sway in an invisible breeze. He found it next to intolerable, the juxtaposition of so much iconography. He experienced this as if everything in the world was somewhere embedded in a place mat or a calendar. Such appropriation was basic to the human process; this fetish of fixing, of setting the permanent imprint of a label was, to his mind, physical response as concomitant of dread, as if everything were in imminent peril of a split and all the darling impressions, the spires and the delphiniums, the ball gowns and dachshunds, might leap into the fissure and out of being.

Lunch, then. He strolled over to the old brasserie in the Jewish quarter where he sat at someone else's usual table. The silk tulips were a permanently fresh representation of decay. The plates were agreeable, the cutlery odd in that the handlework seemed modelled for unknown use. The peckishness he felt himself undergo was, he knew, the somatic rising within him. The ego is a bodily ego, he recalled, the self an organic self: that temporary organisation his being imposed upon its constituents and his name that isolated one object amid the tumult and disorder. He felt the omelette enter him and believed he could detect the foodstuffs assimilated, becoming him. How far from a definition of the word 'hunger' all this was.

Afternoon, recumbent on his hotel balcony, the car roar and the taxi roar and the autobus roar were a crescendo muted to a more possible cacophony by his being at the rear of the building. He could make out in the burn of the gasoline – the shared logical form of the sound waves and the fuel's oxidisation – the second death of the Carboniferous, the feeding earth's absorption reversed to liquid flame then re-expressed as engine idle. Such conjecturing, he conjectured, may create its own conditions or grounds of satisfaction.

He stood bewildered under the stars of the security camera lights, light-instants away from his impromptu boudoir. He imagined to himself an old-master painting in the Louvre: a portrait of the almighty himself as the name *Yahweh* spelt across the sombre heavens in letters of flame. Perhaps this was what Moses saw in the burning bush. Then the young Rimbaud was invented (by the young Rimbaud) to exorcise God by writing him away in verse. Thus is he the sacred icon of the iconoclasts!

In the rectangular room angled obliquely by a lime-coloured street-lighting from the balcony windows, he repeated his own name over and over until it became something wholly new and extraordinary. He sat at the end of the bed, motionless. The moon over Notre Dame was a monstrous full stop.

# Haut Ordure

Nail varnish and the virulent scent of aspiration
bond them to the contemporary.
They have become able,
in the course of their long-drawn-out young lives,
to sacrifice a thousand satisfactions
for twenty correct footfalls on the right catwalk.
Cashmere and the silk of long-dead worms
hang on them in a purposeful disarray.
What they have is the impeccable stance
and a smile from the chef de couture if they are good.
They bang for advancement, bitch without quarter,
smoke endless cigarettes in precisely the same fashion.

# A Dramatic Monologue

*for J*

*"O what can ail thee knight-at-arms*
*alone and palely loitering?"*


Sometime after lunch on the afternoon of April the 11th 1819,
a hundred and ninety years ago to the day in fact,
John Keats walks out of that front door of that house across
    the road there.
He walks down the front path and out of that gate.
He turns right and makes his way towards Hampstead Heath.
He has on an old coat and a scarf to protect his sickly throat.
What he's thinking about, God knows, himself most probably,
or his verse, or his stuckness, which amount to the same thing.

He walks out across the Heath 'Towards Highgate'.
What birds are abroad is not recorded,
a recent nightingale perhaps, preparing itself
not to be born for death. The spring flowers –
mauve crocuses and daffodils – are well into bloom,
as they are, you notice, today; the temperate air hangs
above the heathland like the soft breath of a dryad.

He gets to Millfield Lane at Ken Wood
that 'winds by the side of Lord Mansfield's estate'.
There he encounters two men, one of whom is personally
    known to him:
he is his Demonstrator from his apothecary studies at Guy's.
The other gentleman, he recognizes at once.
Dr Green, the Demonstrator and minor hero of the piece,

sums up the situation and makes the introductions
between the two strangers: *May I present Mr John Keats?* –
*John Keats? The Poet? Well found. How do you do, sir?*
This second man is, well, it's Coleridge!
*Samuel Taylor Coleridge*, S.T.C., the sage of Highgate,
the Ancient Mariner himself. You can see the irony:
this time he's the one who's been waylaid on his promenade.

As the two men go to take their leave of him, Keats can't stand it:
we know, do we not, how passionate he is.
Now this is where we are forced to postulate unknowables:
did Keats feel some licence here suggested by the mariner's rime?
He enquires by a look whether it would be agreeable
that he join them on their walk.
"Yes sir, delighted, do walk with us . . . "
Turns out it is the best thing he ever did in his life.
Hell, it's practically the best thing any poet ever did in any life!

You see it's Coleridge:
Coleridge of the willing suspension of disbelief;
Coleridge, the sadder and the wiser man;
Coleridge the supernatural genius of expostulation.
So, of course, *think about it*, it's Coleridge who does all the talking:
Nightingales, Poetry – Metaphysics – A dream related –
Nightmare – the difference explained between will and Volition
– a dream accompanied by a sense of touch – single and double
touch – Mermaids, Southey believes in them – a Ghost story.
Civil enough, he is, to bid Keats visit him in Highgate.

What d'ya know, a few nights later, for that suffersome throat,
Keats takes a small opium and has a little dream. Sound familiar?
'La Belle Dame sans Merci' comes tripping out.
Sans Merci? *Merci beaucoup*, I'd say! And then the Odes

break from him, then the rest of the Annus Mirabilis
like a waterfall inflamed by a great spring thaw.

But back to that day. The three make their farewells.
Keats walks on a few yards then turns around.
He thinks, he runs back, catches them up again,
gasps, 'Let me carry away the memory, Coleridge,
of having pressed your hand!' They shake.
The kindly April atmosphere lifts a warm sigh, I like to imagine,
much like this soft afternoon of ours here, son.
The flowers continue with their succulent poses,
the birds, a small brown scuffle in the hedgerow.
'There was death in that hand,' says Coleridge to Green.
Keats hurries off to become immortal.
The two men never meet again.

*Keats Grove, April 11th 2009*

# Boy Son

O my homunculus,
your sweet hand which will one day cast down
the handful of soil onto my coffin lid!

# Dead Alsatian in a Vegetable Crate

Like an old overcoat lumped in the damp corner of an attic,
its mass gives off a faint, sweet aroma,
one visible eye like a button beyond a blink.
His ear is folded to the shape of a twisted cuff
and from the gape of his mouth his tongue,
his hanging tongue, continues to evince
his one positive emotion which is glee,
as if, for a last encore, he has just gone through
his entire box of tricks: sit, roll over, play dead.

# Sands

First let me say this: my father never lied.
So it seems strange to me now and yet more obvious in a way
to speak out what happened that day, a day untouched by colour
in the indifferent mustering of what sun there was.
The stinging wind would blow sand in your nose
and in your eyes so you would look as if you'd been crying
(which you definitely *hadn't* been at that age),
or off the raked roof of Sand Dunes, the bungalow we'd rented
for a damp few days in a wet approximation of a place.

That day, I look into the lipstick red telephone box,
he presses button A and something drops.
His voice seems to stray beyond it,
beyond our playground crazy-golf scene;
his eyes follow. He throws his head back, grins
then laughs that rude word. The other end, I cannot hear,
but he turns and clocks me watching him:
the smile straightens, a crease cuts itself into his forehead.

'Nothing. Just sand in his eyes from kiddie-golf,'
I later hear him tell my mother
in words culled of sense as if mustered by the wind.
But today – long since everything shifted
like a downslope in the dunes
when one foot slips one way and the other
takes its own insane ellipsis, meets only the elision
of what's solid, what falls away –
what I *can* say is: go a few moments back on that day
when the rain iterated to more rain as we trudged,
two half-soaked conspirators in just what, I didn't know,

as we walked back down our lane I'd never seen before
under the fractious wind that concerned itself
merely with trying to blow the roofs off the bungalows,
but wasn't able to (just), as my mother,
eyes slitted against the air, looked at me,
looked at my father and asked what the matter was
because I looked as if I'd been crying,
which I definitely had not been.

# That Sweet Before Emotion

This is yesterday's tomorrow when middle-aged men
slide into hot tubs to ease the slump
of their feckless muscles. Happy again
to reel in an old warmth, and relive short forays of adventure.
Once more they have fathers to tell their days to:
the Navaho raid, the Viking sea-battle,
Batman plunged into the deep night
to pluck jailbirds back to jail.
Or mothers: the scent of rosewater that lingers
in pools above a crisply made-up bed
and settles on a forehead
before she pulls the veil across the night.
They remember it all, sorry for everything.